WARSHIP PICTORIAL #22

# *United States Navy*

# USS TICONDEROGA CV/CVA/CVS-14

**by Steve Wiper**

*The* Ticonderoga *departing the Norfolk Navy Yard, May 30, 1944.*

**CLASSIC WARSHIPS PUBLISHING**
P. O. Box 57591 • Tucson, AZ. 85732 • USA
Web Site: www.classicwarships.com • Ph/Fx (520)748-2992

**ISBN 0-9745687-2-4**

Printed by Arizona Lithographers, Tucson, Arizona

# History of the USS Ticonderoga CV / CVA / CVS-14

The fourth *Ticonderoga (CV-14)* was laid down as the *Hancock* on February 1, 1943 at Newport News, Va., by the Newport News Shipbuilding & Dry Dock Co. The warship was renamed *Ticonderoga* on May 1, 1943, and launched on February 7, 1944. She was commissioned at the Norfolk Navy Yard on May 8, 1944, Capt. Dixie Kiefer in command. She was the lead ship in a modified design of the *Essex* class with an extended bow accommodating two 40 mm quadruple AA mounts instead of one as in the previous class.

*Ticonderoga* remained at Norfolk for almost two months outfitting and embarking Air Group 80. On June 26, 1944, the carrier headed for the British West Indies. She conducted air operations and drills en route and reached Port of Spain, Trinidad, on the 30th For the next 15 days, *Ticonderoga* trained intensively to form her air group and crew into an efficient wartime team.

She departed the West Indies on July 16, 1944 and headed back to Norfolk where she arrived on the 22nd Eight days later, the carrier headed for Panama. She transited the canal on September 4th and steamed up the coast to San Diego, CA. the following day. On the 13th the carrier moored at San Diego where she loaded provisions, fuel, aviation gas, and an additional 77 planes, as well as the Marine Corps aviation and defense units that went with them. On the 19th she sailed for Hawaii and the Pacific Theater of Operations, where she arrived five days later.

*Ticonderoga* remained at Pearl Harbor for almost a month. She and *Carina (AK-74)* conducted experiments in the underway transfer of aviation bombs from cargo ship to aircraft carrier. Following those tests, she conducted air operations, day and night landings and antiaircraft defense drills until October 18th, when she departed Pearl Harbor and headed for the western Pacific.

After a brief stop at Eniwetok, *Ticonderoga* arrived at the Ulithi Atoll in the Western Carolines on October 29, 1944. There she embarked Rear Admiral A. W. Radford, Commander, Carrier Division 6, and joined Task Force (TF) 38 as a unit of Rear Admiral Frederick C. Sherman's Task Group (TG) 38.3.

The carrier sortied from Ulithi with TF-38 on November 2, 1944. She joined the other carriers as they resumed their extended air cover for the ground forces capturing Leyte. She launched her first air strike on the morning of November 5th. The planes of her air group spent the next two days pummeling enemy shipping near Luzon and air installations on that island. Her aircraft bombed and strafed the airfields at Zablan, Mandaluyong, and Pasig. They also joined those of other carriers in sending the Japanese heavy cruiser *Nachi* to a watery resting place in Manila Bay. In addition, *Ticonderoga* pilots claimed six Japanese aircraft shot down and one destroyed on the ground, as well as 23 others damaged.

Around 1600hrs on the 5th, the Japanese retaliated by sending up a flight of planes piloted by members of the suicide corps dubbed "Kamikaze, or Divine Wind," in honor of the typhoon that had destroyed a Chinese invasion fleet four centuries previously. Two of the Japanese suicide planes succeeded in slipping through the American combat air patrol and anti-aircraft fire to crash into the *Lexington (CV-16). Ticonderoga* emerged from that airborne banzai charge unscathed and claimed a tally of two planes shot down.

On November 6th, the carrier launched two fighter sweeps and two bombing strikes against the Luzon airfields and enemy shipping in the vicinity. Her airmen returned later that day claiming the destruction of 35 Japanese aircraft and attacks on six enemy ships in Manila Bay. After recovering her aircraft, the carrier retired to the east for a fueling rendezvous.

She refueled and received replacement planes on the 7th and then headed back to continue pounding enemy forces in the Philippines. Early on the morning of November 11, 1944, her planes combined with others of TF-38 to attack a Japanese reinforcement convoy, just as it was preparing to enter Ormoc Bay from the Camotes Sea. Together, the aircraft accounted for all the enemy transports and four of the seven escorting destroyers.

On the 12th and 13th, *Ticonderoga* and her sisters launched strikes at Luzon air fields and docks and shipping around Manila. This raid tallied an impressive score. They sank the Japanese light cruiser *Kiso*, four destroyers, and seven merchant ships. At the conclusion of the raid, TF-38 retired eastward for a refueling breather. *Ticonderoga* and the rest of TG-38.3 continued east to Ulithi where they arrived on November 17th to replenish, refuel, and rearm.

On November 22nd, the aircraft carrier departed Ulithi once more and steamed back toward the Philippines. Three days later, she launched air strikes on central Luzon and adjacent waters. Her pilots finished off the Imperial Japanese Navy (IJN) heavy cruiser *Kumano*, damaged earlier in the Battle off Samar. Later, they attacked an enemy convoy about 15 miles southwest of *Kumano's* position in Dasol Bay. Of this convoy, the light cruiser *Yasoshima* (ex-Chinese *P'ing Hai*), a merchantman, and three landing ships went to the bottom. *Ticonderoga's* air group rounded out their day of destruction with an aerial rampage which cost the Japanese 15 planes shot down and 11 destroyed on the ground.

While her air group busily pounded the Japanese, *Ticonderoga's* ship's company also made their presence felt. Just after noon, a torpedo launched by an enemy plane broached in *Langley's (CVL-27)* wake to announce the approach of an air raid . *Ticonderoga's* gunners raced to their battle stations as the raiders made both conventional and suicide attacks on the task group. Her sister ship *Essex (CV-9)* erupted in flames when one of the kamikazes crashed into her. When a second suicide plane tried to finish off the stricken carrier, *Ticonderoga's* gunners joined those firing from other ships in cutting off his approach abruptly short. That afternoon, while damage control parties dressed *Essex's* wounds, *Ticonderoga* extended her hospitality to that damaged carrier's homeless airmen as well as to *USS Intrepid (CV-11)* pilots in similar straits. The following day, TF-38 retired to the east.

TF 38 steamed out of Ulithi again on December 11, 1944, and headed for the Philippines. *Ticonderoga* arrived at the launch point early in the afternoon of the 13th and sent her planes aloft to blanket Japanese airbases on Luzon while Army planes took care of those in the central Philippines. For three days, *Ticonderoga* airmen and their comrades wreaked havoc with a storm of destruction on enemy airfields.

She withdrew on the 16th with the rest of TF-38 in search of a fueling rendezvous. While attempting to find calmer waters in which to refuel, TF-38 steamed directly through a violent, but unheralded, typhoon. Though the storm cost Admiral Halsey's force three destroyers and over 800 lives, *Ticonderoga* and the other carriers managed to ride it out with a minimum of damage. Having survived the tempest's fury, *Ticonderoga* returned to Ulithi on Christmas Eve.

Repairs necessary after the typhoon kept TF-38 in the anchorage almost until the end of the month. The carriers did not return to sea until December 30, 1944, when they steamed north to hit Formosa and Luzon in preparation for the landings on the latter island at Lingayen Gulf. Severe weather limited the Formosa strikes on January 3rd and 4th, 1945 and, in all likelihood, obviated the need for them. The warships refueled at sea on the 5th. Despite rough weather on the 6th, the strikes on Luzon airfields were carried out. That day, *Ticonderoga's* airmen and their colleagues of the other air groups increased their score by another 32 enemy planes. The 7th brought more strikes on Luzon installations. After a fueling rendezvous on the 8th., *Ticonderoga* sped north at night to get into position to blanket Japanese airfields in the Ryukyu Islands during the Lingayen assault the following morning. However, foul weather, the bugaboo of TF-38 during the winter of 1944 and 1945, forced TG-38.3 to abandon the strikes on the Ryukyu airfields and join TG-38.2 in pounding Formosa.

During the night of January 9th and 10th, 1945, TF-38 steamed boldly through the Luzon Strait and then headed generally southwest, diagonally across the South China Sea. *Ticonderoga* provided combat air patrol coverage on the 11th and helped to bring down four enemy planes which attempted to attack the formation. Otherwise, the carriers and their escorts proceeded unmolested to a point some 150 to 200 miles off the coast of Indochina.

On January 12th, TF-38 launched their approximately 850 planes and made a series of anti-shipping sweeps during which they sank 44 ships, totaling over 130,000 tons. After recovering aircraft in the late afternoon, the carriers moved off to the northeast. Heavy weather hindered refueling operations on the 13th and 14th, and air searches failed to turn up any tempting targets. On the 15th, fighters swept Japanese airfields on the Chinese coast while the flattops headed for a position from which to strike Hong Kong. The following morning, they launched anti-shipping bombing raids and fighter sweeps of air installations. Weather prevented air operations on January 17th and again made refueling difficult. It worsened the next day and stopped replenishment operations altogether, so that they were not finally concluded until the 19th. The force then steamed generally northward to retransit Luzon Strait via Balintang Channel.

The three task groups of TF-38 completed their transit during the night of January 20th and 21st. The next morning, their planes hit airfields on Formosa, in the Pescadores, and at Sakishima Gunto. The good flying weather brought mixed blessings. While it allowed American flight operations to continue through the day, it also brought new gusts of the "Divine Wind." Just after noon, a single-engine Japanese plane scored a hit on *Langley* with a glide-bombing attack. Seconds later, a kamikaze swooped out of the clouds and plunged toward *Ticonderoga*. He crashed through her flight deck abreast of the No. 2 5 in./38 cal. mount, and his bomb exploded just above her hangar deck. Several planes stowed nearby erupted into flames. Death and destruction abounded, but the ship's company fought valiantly to save the threatened carrier. Capt. Kiefer conned his ship smartly. First, he changed course to keep the wind from fanning the blaze. Then, he ordered magazines and other compartments flooded to prevent further explosions and to correct a 10° starboard list. Finally, he instructed the damage control party to continue flooding compartments on *Ticonderoga's* port side. That operation induced a 10° port list which neatly dumped the fire overboard! Fire fighters and plane handlers completed the job by dousing the flames and jettisoning burning aircraft.

Damaged or burning ships often attract predators. *Ticonderoga* was no exception. The other kamikazes pounced on her like a school of sharks in a feeding frenzy. Her anti-aircraft gunners struck back with desperate but methodical ferocity and quickly swatted three of her tormentors into the sea. A fourth plane slipped through her barrage and smashed into the carrier's starboard side near the island. His bomb set more aircraft on fire, riddled her flight deck, and injured or killed another 100 sailors, including Capt. Kiefer. Yet, *Ticonderoga's* crew refused to submit. Spared further attacks, they brought her fires completely under control not long after 1400hrs and *Ticonderoga* retired painfully.

The stricken carrier arrived at Ulithi on January 24, 1945, but remained there only long enough to move her wounded to hospital ship *USS Samaritan (AH-10)*, to transfer her air group to *USS Hancock (CV-19)*, and to embark passengers bound for home. The *Ticonderoga* cleared the lagoon on January 28th and headed for the United States. The warship stopped briefly at Pearl Harbor en route to the Puget Sound Naval Shipyard, where she arrived on February 15, 1945.

Her repairs were completed on April 20th, and she cleared Puget Sound the following day for the Alameda Naval Air Station, San Francisco Bay. After embarking passengers and aircraft bound for Hawaii, the carrier headed for Pearl Harbor where she arrived on May 1st. The next day, Air Group 87 came on board and for the next week trained in preparation for the carrier's return to combat. *Ticonderoga* stood out of Pearl Harbor and steamed for the western Pacific. En route to Ulithi, she launched her planes for what amounted to training strikes on Japanese held Taroa in the Marshall Island Group. On May 22nd the warship arrived in Ulithi and rejoined the Fast Carrier Task Force as an element of Rear Admiral Radford's TG-58.4.

Two days after her arrival, *Ticonderoga* sortied from Ulithi with TF-58 and headed north to spend the last weeks of the war in Japanese home waters. Three days out, Admiral Halsey relieved Admiral Spruance, the 5th Fleet reverted back to 3d Fleet, and TF-58 became TF-38 again for the duration. On June 2nd and 3rd, *Ticonderoga* fighters struck at airfields on Kyushu in an effort to neutralize the remnants of Japanese air power, particularly the Kamikaze Corps, and to relieve the pressure on American forces at Okinawa.

During the following two days, *Ticonderoga* rode out her second typhoon in less than six months and emerged relatively unscathed. On June 6th she provided combat air patrol cover for a refueling rendezvous, during which four of her fighters intercepted and destroyed three Okinawa-bound kamikazes. That evening, she steamed off at high speed with TG-38.4 to conduct a fighter sweep of air-fields on southern Kyushu on June 8th. *Ticonderoga's* planes then joined in the aerial bombardment of Minami Daito Shima and Kita Daito Shima before the carrier headed for Leyte where she arrived on the 13th.

During the two week rest and replenishment period (R & R) she enjoyed at Leyte, *Ticonderoga* changed task organizations from TG-38.4 to Rear Admiral Gerald F. Bogan's TG-38.3. On July 1st she departed Leyte with TF-38 and headed north to resume raids on Japan. Two days later, a damaged reduction gear forced her into Apra Harbor, Guam, for repairs. She remained there until July 19, 1945, when she steamed off to rejoin TF-38 and resume her role in the war against Japan.

On July 24th, *Ticonderoga's* planes joined those of other fast carriers in striking ships in the Inland Sea and airfields at Nagoya, Osaka and Miko, Japan. During those raids, TF-38 planes found the sad remnants of the once-mighty Imperial Japanese Navy and sunk battleships *Ise*, *Hyuga*, and *Haruna* as well as an escort carrier, *Kaiyo*, and two heavy cruisers, *Aoba* and *Tone*. On July 28th, her aircraft directed their efforts toward the Kure Naval Base, where they pounded an aircraft carrier, three cruisers, a destroyer, and a submarine. Her aircraft then shifted their attention to the industrial area of central Honshu on the 30th, then to northern Honshu and Hokkaido on August 9th and 10th The latter attacks thoroughly destroyed the marshaling area for a planned airborne suicide raid on the B-29 bases in the Marianas. On the 13th and 14th, her planes returned to the Tokyo area and helped to subject the Japanese capital to another severe working over.

The two atomic bombs dropped on Hiroshima and Nagasaki on the 6th. and 9th. of August, convinced the Japanese leader, Emperor Hirohito of the futility of continued resistance. On the morning of August 15th, *Ticonderoga* launched another strike against Tokyo. During or just after that attack, word reached TF-38 to the effect that Japan had capitulated.

The shock of peace, though not so abrupt as that of war almost four years previously, took some getting used to. *Ticonderoga* and her sister ships remained on a full war footing. She continued patrols over Japanese territory and sent reconnaissance flights in search of camps containing Allied prisoners of war so that air-dropped supplies could be rushed to them. On September 6th, four days after the formal surrender ceremony on board the *USS Missouri (BB-63), Ticonderoga* entered Tokyo Bay as part of the Occupation Fleet.

Her arrival at Tokyo ended one phase of her career and began another. She embarked homeward bound passengers and put to sea again on September 20, 1945. After a stop in Pearl Harbor, the carrier reached Alameda, California, on October 5th. She disembarked her passengers and unloaded cargo before heading out on the 9th to pick up another group of veterans at Pearl Harbor.

*Ticonderoga* delivered over a thousand soldiers and sailors to Tacoma, Washington, and remained there through the 28th for the National Navy Day celebration. On October 29th, the carrier departed Tacoma and headed back to Alameda. En route, all of the planes of Air Group 87 were transferred ashore so that the carrier could be altered to accommodate additional passengers in the "Magic Carpet" voyages to follow. Following the completion of those modifications at the Pearl Harbor Naval Shipyard in November 1945, the warship headed for the Philippines and arrived at Samar on November 20th. She returned to Alameda on December 6th with almost 4,000 returning servicemen. The carrier made one more "Magic Carpet" from December 1945 through January 1946 before entering the Puget Sound Naval Shipyard to prepare for inactivation. Almost a year later on January 9, 1947, *USS Ticonderoga CV-14* was placed out of commission and berthed with the Bremerton Group of the Pacific Reserve Fleet.

On January 31, 1952, *Ticonderoga* came out of reserve and went into reduced commission for the transit from Bremerton to New York. She departed Puget Sound on February 27th and reached New York on April 1st. Three days later, she was decommissioned at the New York Naval Shipyard to begin an extensive conversion. This refit took place from April 15, 1952 to October 1, 1954. On October 1, 1952, near the beginning of that refit, the *Ticonderoga* was reclassified as an Attack Aircraft Carrier (CVA). During the ensuing 29 months, the carrier received numerous modifications, such as improved steam catapults to launch jets, a new nylon crash barricade, a new deck edge elevator, improved anti-aircraft armament and the latest electronic and fire control equipment necessary for her to become an integral unit of the fleet. On September 11, 1954, *USS Ticonderoga CVA-14* was recommissioned at New York, commanded by Capt. William A. Schoech.

In January 1955, the carrier shifted to her new home port at Norfolk, Virginia, where she arrived on the 6th. Over the next month, she conducted carrier qualifications with Air Group 6 in the Virginia Capes operating area. On February 3rd, she stood out of Hampton Roads for a shakedown cruise near Cuba, after which she returned via Norfolk to New York for additional alterations. During the late summer, the warship resumed carrier qualifications in the Virginia capes area.

After a visit to Philadelphia early in September 1955, she participated in tests of three new planes, the A4D-1 Skyhawk, the F4D-1 Skyray, and the F3H-2N Demon. *Ticonderoga* then returned to normal operations along the east coast until November 4th when she departed Mayport, Florida, and headed for Europe. She relieved *USS Intrepid CVA-11* at Gibraltar 10 days later and cruised the length of the Mediterranean during the following eight months. On August 2, 1956, *Ticonderoga* returned to Norfolk and entered the shipyard to receive an angled flight deck and an enclosed hurricane bow. This modernization transpired from August 17, 1956 to April 1, 1957.

In April, *Ticonderoga* got underway for her new home port, Alameda, California. She reached her destination on May 30th, underwent repairs, and finished out the summer with operations off the California coast. On September 16th, she stood out of San Francisco Bay and steamed for the Far East. En route, she stopped at Pearl Harbor before continuing west to Yokosuka, Japan, where she arrived on October 15th. For six months, *Ticonderoga* cruised Oriental waters from Japan in the north to the Philippines in the south. She would then return to the United States, arriving at Alameda on April 25, 1958, completing her first deployment to the western Pacific since recommissioning.

Between 1958 and 1963, the *Ticonderoga* shifted homeport to San Diego, California and made four more peacetime deployments to the western Pacific. During each, she conducted training operations with other units of the 7th Fleet and made goodwill and liberty port calls throughout the Far East. Early in 1964, she began preparations for her sixth cruise to the western Pacific and, following exercises off the west coast of the United States and the Hawaiian Islands, the carrier cleared Pearl Harbor on May 4th, 1964, for what began as another peaceful tour of duty in the Far East. The first three months of that deployment brought normal operations, training and port calls. However, on August 2nd, while operating in international waters in the Gulf of Tonkin, Vietnam, the destroyer *USS Maddox (DD-731)* reported being attacked by units of the North Vietnamese Navy. Within minutes of her receipt of the message, *Ticonderoga* dispatched four, rocket-armed F8E Crusaders to the destroyer's assistance.

Two days later, late in the evening of August 4th, *Ticonderoga* received urgent requests from the destroyer *Turner Joy (DD-951)*, by then on patrol with *Maddox,* for air support in resisting what the destroyer alleged to be another torpedo boat foray. The carrier again launched planes to aid the American surface ships, and *Turner Joy* directed them. The US Navy surface ships believed it had sunk two boats and damaged another pair. The air group did not make contact with any hostile vessels.

President Johnson responded with a reprisal to what he felt at the time to be two unprovoked attacks on American seapower and ordered retaliatory air strikes on selected North Vietnamese motor torpedo boat bases. On August 5th, *Ticonderoga* and *USS Constellation (CV-46)* launched 60 sorties against four bases and their supporting oil storage facilities. Those attacks reportedly resulted in the destruction of 25 PT type boats, severe damage to the bases, and almost complete razing of the oil storage depot. For her quick reaction and successful combat actions on those three occasions, *Ticonderoga* received the Navy Unit

Commendation.

After a return visit to Japan in September 1964, the aircraft carrier resumed normal operations in the South China Sea until winding up the deployment late in that year. She returned to her homeport, the Naval Air Station, North Island, in San Diego, California, on December 15, 1964. Following post-deployment and holiday stand down, *Ticonderoga* moved to the Hunter's Point Naval Shipyard on January 27, 1965 to begin a five month overhaul.

She completed repairs in June 1965 and spent the summer operating along the coast of southern California. On September 28th, the aircraft carrier put to sea for another deployment to the Orient. She spent some time in the Hawaiian Islands for an operational readiness exercise and then continued on to the Far East. She reached "Dixie Station" (waters off South Vietnam) on November 5th. and immediately began combat air operations.

*Ticonderoga's* winter deployment of 1965 and 1966 was her first complete combat tour of duty during American involvement in the Vietnam War. During her six months in the Far East, the carrier spent a total of 116 days in air operations off the coast of Vietnam dividing her time almost evenly between "Dixie" and "Yankee Stations," the carrier operating areas off South and North Vietnam, respectively. Her air group delivered over 8,000 tons of ordnance in more than 10,000 combat sorties, with a loss of 16 planes, but only 5 pilots. For the most part, her aircraft hit enemy installations in North Vietnam and interdicted supply routes into South Vietnam, including river-borne and coastal junk and sampan traffic as well as roads, bridges, and trucks on land. Specifically, they claimed the destruction of 35 bridges as well as numerous warehouses, barracks, trucks, boats, and railroad cars and severe damage to a major North Vietnamese thermal power plant located at Uong Bi north of Haiphong. After a stop at Sasebo, Japan, from April 25 to May 3, 1966, the warship put to sea to return to the United States. On May 13th she pulled into port at San Diego, California to end that deployment.

Following repairs she steamed out of San Diego on July 9, 1966, to begin a routine round of west coast training operations. Those and similar operations continued until October 15th when *Ticonderoga* departed San Diego, bound via Hawaii for the western Pacific Ocean. The carrier reached Yokosuka, Japan, on October 30th and remained there until November 5th, when she headed south for an overnight stop at Subic Bay in the Philippines on the 10th and 11th. On the 13th *Ticonderoga* arrived in the Gulf of Tonkin (Yankee Station) and began the first of three combat tours during her 1966-67 deployment. She launched 11,650 combat sorties, all against enemy targets located in North Vietnam. Again, her primary targets were logistics and communications lines and transportation facilities. For their overall efforts in the conduct of day and night strikes on enemy targets, *Ticonderoga* and her air group earned their second Navy Unit Commendation. She completed her final line period on April 27, 1967 and returned to Yokosuka, from which she departed again on May 19th to return to the United States. Ten days later, the carrier entered San Diego and began a one month post-deployment stand-down. At the beginning of July, the warship shifted to Bremerton, where she entered the Puget Sound Naval Shipyard for two months of repairs.

Upon the completion of yard work, she departed Bremerton on September 6, 1967 and steamed south for training operations off the coast of southern California. On 28 December, *Ticonderoga* sailed for her fourth combat deployment to the waters off the Indochinese coast. She made port at Yokosuka on January 17, 1968 and after two days of upkeep continued on to the Gulf of Tonkin where she arrived on "Yankee Station" on the 26th and began combat operations. Between January and July, 1968, *Ticonderoga* was on the line off the coast of Vietnam for five separate periods totaling 120 days of combat duty. During that time, her air wing flew just over 13,000 combat sorties against North Vietnamese and Viet Cong forces, most frequently in the continuing attempts to interdict the enemy lines of supply. In mid-April, following her second line period, she made a port visit to Singapore and then, after upkeep at Subic Bay, returned to duty off Vietnam. On July 9th, during her fifth and final line period, Lt. Comdr. J. B. Nichols claimed *Ticonderoga's* first MiG shot down (Soviet designed fighter aircraft flown by the Communist Chinese in support of North Vietnam). The carrier completed that line period and entered Subic Bay, Manila, the Philippines, for upkeep on July 25, 1968.

At sometime during the first six months of 1968, *Ticonderoga* operated of the coast of North Korea due to the hostile takeover of the reconnaissance ship *USS Pueblo AGER-2*. The *Pueblo* was fired upon by North Korean patrol boats and boarded on January 23, 1968, killing one USN serviceman and capturing and held hostage the remainder of the 82 man crew. At some point after that date, the *"Tico"* patrolled off the coast of North Korea for a brief period.

On July 27, she headed north to Yokosuka, Japan, where she spent a week for upkeep and briefings before heading back to the United States on August 7th. *Ticonderoga* reached San Diego on the 17th and disembarked her air group. On the 22nd, she entered the Long Beach Naval Shipyard, California, for post-deployment repairs. She completed those repairs on October 21st, conducted sea trials on the 28th and 29th, and began routine operations out of San Diego early in November. For the remainder of the year, she conducted refresher training and carrier qualifications along the coast of southern California.

During January 1969, *Ticonderoga* made preparations for her fifth consecutive combat deployment to the southeast Asia operations area. On February 1st she cleared San Diego and headed west. After a brief stop at Pearl Harbor a week later, she continued her voyage to Yokosuka, Japan, where she arrived on the 20th. The carrier departed Yokosuka on the 28th for the coast of Vietnam where she arrived on March 4th. Over the next four months, *Ticonderoga* served four periods on the line off Vietnam, interdicting communist supply lines and making strikes against their positions.

During her second line period her tour of duty off Vietnam came to an abrupt end on April 16th when she was shifted north to the Sea of Japan. North Korean aircraft had shot down a Navy reconnaissance plane in the area, and *Ticonderoga* was called upon to beef up the forces assigned to the vicinity. However, the crisis abated, and *Ticonderoga* entered Subic Bay on April 27th for upkeep. On May 8th she departed the Philippines to return to "Yankee Station" and resumed interdiction operations. Between her third and fourth line periods, the carrier also visited Sasebo, Japan and the port of Hong Kong.

The aircraft carrier took station off Vietnam for her last line period of the deployment on June 26, 1969, and there followed 37 more days of highly successful air sorties against enemy targets. Following that tour, she joined TF-71 in the Sea of Japan for the remainder of the deployment. *Ticonderoga* received her third Navy Unit Commendation for her operations during this highly successful deployment when she left Subic Bay on September 4, 1969, bound for the west coast of the United States.

*Ticonderoga* arrived in San Diego on September 18th. After almost a month of post-deployment stand-down, she moved to the Long Beach Naval Shipyard in mid October to begin conversion to an anti-submarine warfare (ASW) aircraft carrier. Overhaul and conversion work began on October 20th and she was redesignated *USS Ticonderoga CVS-14* on the 21st. She completed that overhaul and conversion on May 28, 1970 and conducted exercises out of Long Beach off the west coast for most of June 1970. On the 26th, the new ASW support carrier entered her new home port, San Diego. During July and August, she conducted refresher training, refresher air operations, and carrier landing qualifications. The warship operated off the California coast for the remainder of the year and participated in two exercises, HUKASWEX 4-70 late in October and COMPUTEX 23-70 between November 30th and December 3, 1970.

During the remainder of her active career, *Ticonderoga* made two more deployments to the Far East. Because of her change in mission, neither tour of duty included combat operations off Vietnam. Both deployments included training exercises in the Sea of Japan with ships of the Japanese Maritime Self Defense Force. The first of these two cruises also brought operations in the Indian Ocean with units of the Thai Navy and a transit of Sunda Strait during which a ceremony was held to commemorate the losses of the heavy cruiser *USS Houston (CA-30)* and the Australian light cruiser *HMAS Perth* in a very one sided battle against the Japanese Navy during World War Two, early in 1942.

In between these two last deployments, she operated in the eastern Pacific Ocean and participated in the recovery of the Apollo 16 moon mission capsule and astronauts near American Samoa during April 1972. The second deployment came in the summer of 1972, and in addition to the training exercises in the Sea of Japan, *Ticonderoga* also joined ASW training operations in the South China Sea. That fall, she returned to the eastern Pacific and in November 1972 practiced for the recovery of Apollo 17. The next month, *Ticonderoga* recovered her second set of space voyagers near American Samoa. The carrier then headed back to San Diego where she arrived on December 28, 1972.

*Ticonderoga* remained active for nine more months, operating out of San Diego. During that time, *CVS-14* was the primary recovery vessel for the *Skylab II* astronauts, who returned to Earth on June 22, 1973. *Ticonderoga* then made preparations for inactivation. On September 1, 1973, the aircraft carrier was decommissioned after a board of inspection and survey found her to be unfit for further naval service. Her name was struck from the Navy list on November 16, 1973, and arrangements were begun to sell her for scrapping. She was sold on September 16, 1974.

The *Ticonderoga* received five battle stars during World War II and three Navy Unit Commendations, one Meritorious Unit Commendation, and 12 battle stars during the Vietnam War.

CV-14 *during launching on February 7, 1944, at the Newport News Shipbuilding and Dry Dock Co.*

*Just after launching, the* CV-14 *was pushed into the fitting out basin at Newport News Shipbuilding and Dry Dock Company's shipyard. The warship's anti-aircraft (AA) weapons, directors, radar, and the rest of the island structure were fitted at that time. At the date of this photograph, the vessel was painted overall with a green primer known as 84-D.*

*The image on the previous page to the left was taken on April 16, 1944, in a dry dock at the NNS&DD Co. shipyard, as the vessel underwent a final hull inspection prior to commissioning. The photograph below was also taken on the same day as the* CV-14 *was floated into the dry dock. Note that the carrier had been painted with her dazzle camouflage pattern at that time. To have an appreciation of the size and weight of one of these warships, the anchor seen hanging at the bow of this vessel weighed 40,000 lbs.*

*In this photograph, also taken on April 7, 1944 the* CV-14 *was refloated in the dry dock and the dock gate was just beginning to open. Note the pair of quadruple 40 mm AA mounts on the stern and the single 20 mm AA mounts fitted just below the flight deck edge.*

*The three aerial photographs on this and the opposite page were all taken on May 30, 1944, shortly after* Ticonderoga's *commissioning. Her air group did not arrive until a few weeks after the date of these photographs. The two images on the opposite page show the unique notch in the flight deck to port. This was constructed to allow clearance for a third Mk. 37 director, but it was determined that the unit would interfere with flight deck operations and was therefor never fitted.*

*Both of the photographs on this page were taken on the day of the commissioning of the USS Ticonderoga CV-14 on May 8, 1944, at the NNS&DD Co. shipyard. Her dazzle camouflage pattern was known as Measure 33-Design 10A (Ms. 33-10A). The colors used on the ships vertical surfaces were Navy Blue (5-D), Ocean Gray (5-0) and Light Gray (5-L). Steel decks and other horizontal steel surfaces were painted Deck Blue (20-B). The Douglas Fir wood planking covering the flight deck was stained with Blue Flight Deck Stain #21.*

*Note that the camouflage pattern was different on the port side than that on the starboard side, pictured above.*

*The image above is of the port side of the island structure, as seen from across the flight deck. This photograph was taken on April 22, 1944, shortly before the* Ticonderoga's *commissioning. The small ovals with the numbers and letters mark the paint colors used in her camouflage pattern. Light Gray is marked with its US Navy nomenclature of "5-L", while Ocean Gray and Navy Blue are marked with "5-O" and "5-N", respectively.*

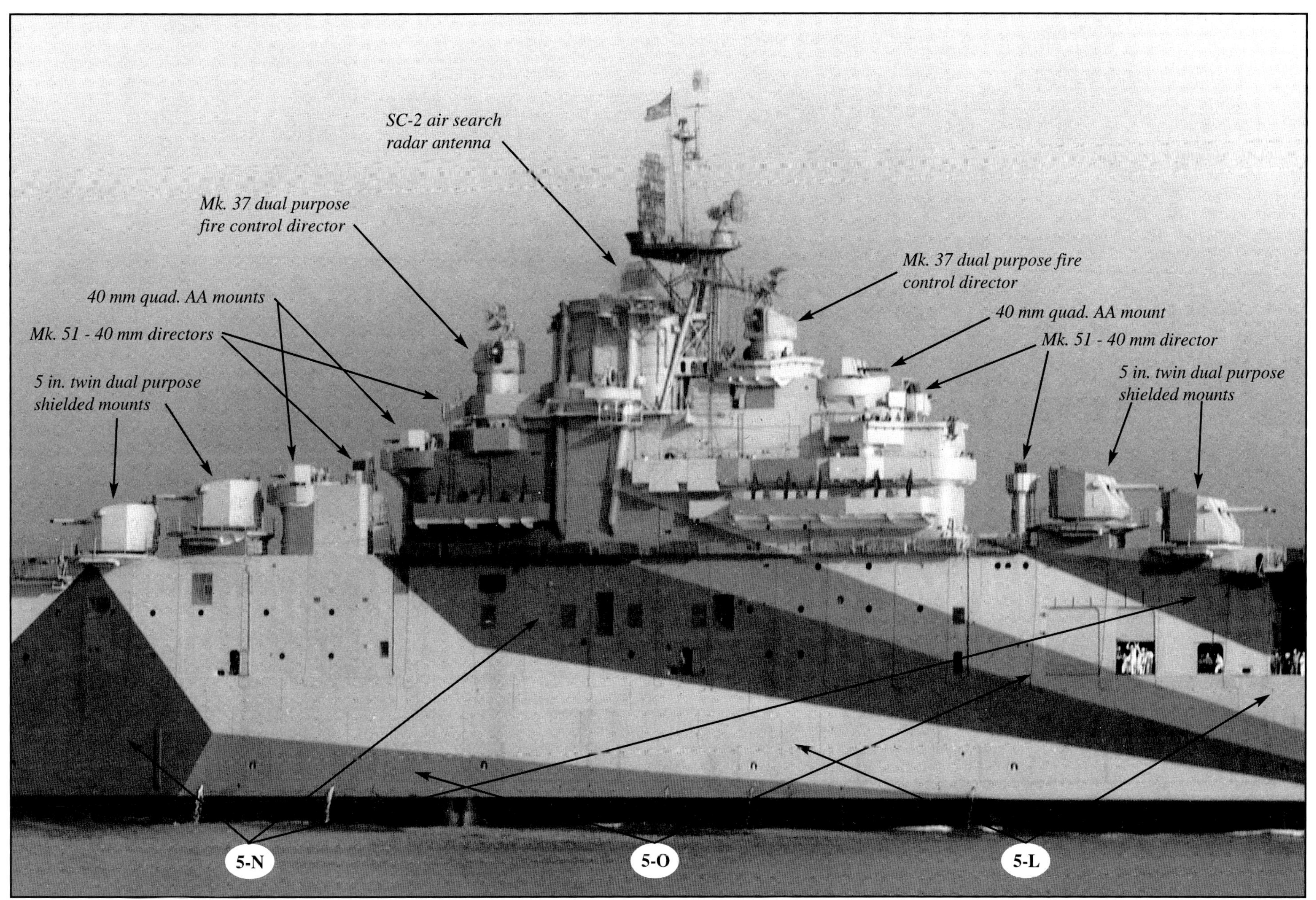


*This view of the starboard side of the island structure was taken on May 8, 1944, on the day of* Ticonderoga's *commissioning.*

*The photograph above was also taken on May 30, 1944, while at the Norfolk Navy Yard during the time of her shakedown cruises out into the Atlantic Ocean. These short journeys were to test her propulsion machinery and to calibrate her compasses. She still did not have her air group aboard at the time this image was taken. This is also a good view of her Ms. 33-10A camouflage pattern.*

*The aerial image below is another photograph taken on May 30, 1944. The wood planked flight deck was stained a dark blue, with the vessel number painted with Dull Black (BK) and the dashed lines were painted with light gray. Note the deck edge elevator on the port side, opposite the island structure, in the stowed position.*

*In this bow view, a pair of 40 mm quad mounts are visible, as well as the pair of catapults installed in the forward flight deck.*

*In this stern view, a pair of 40 mm quad mounts are visible on the fantail and on the port side, but none to starboard aft of the island.*

*This top image of the* Ticonderoga *was taken on June 30, 1944, with Air Group 80 embarked. They would train off of the island of Trinidad for two weeks, where this photograph was taken. Note the port side camouflage pattern was different that that on the starboard side.*

*Another aerial photograph of the "Tico", taken June 30, 1944, this time showing the starboard side with her Ms. 33-10A camouflage and her air group aboard.*

*The lower photograph was taken later on the same date, while the aircraft carrier was recovering her air group. There is a TBM Avenger torpedo bomber in flight in front of the island. Note the aircraft parked at the forward end of the flight deck. This was done to allow aircraft recovery and keep ready aircraft on the flight deck to speed an emergency launch in case the warship was in danger.*

Helldiver

Avenger

Hellcat

*Both of the photographs on this page were taken as the* Ticonderoga *was departing the Norfolk Navy Base on June 26, 1944, bound for Trinidad in the British West Indies. Air Group 80 conducted intensive air operation training en route to Port of Spain, the main anchorage at Trinidad. The aircraft visible on her flight deck are Grumman F6F Hellcat fighters, Grumman TBM Avenger torpedo-bombers, and Curtiss SB2C Helldiver dive-bombers. At this time the "Tico", as she was known by her crew, carried an exceptionally large aircraft complement of 117 planes. Some of these must have been stowed as spares in the rafters inside the hangar, below the flight deck. In the image above the four tall masts on the starboard edge of the flight deck, two forward and two aft, are the warship's radio mast.*

*Air operations on June 28, 1944, while en route to Port of Spain, Trinidad. Air Group 80 trained for four days while this journey was underway. The flight deck crew was in the process of preparing to launch the Hellcat fighters in the foreground of this image.*

*The photograph to the left shows the crowded flight deck conditions forward during aircraft recovery operations. The aircraft in the foreground were TBMs. The primary image on this page shows a TBM that had a bad landing, dated July 11, 1944. The aircraft's landing gear had become entangled in the flight deck landing arrestor wires and nosed over into the wooden deck. This photograph was snapped just as the plane stood on its nose and came to a stop. Accidents like this were not uncommon and were very dangerous for the flight deck crew.*

*"Tico" is refueling an escort,* USS Broome DD-210, *an old* Clemson *class destroyer built at the end of World War One*

*Older four stack destroyers like this were used as escorts and long range patrol vessels in back water areas to free up the new destroyers for front line duty.*

*This photograph of a Curtiss SB2C Helldiver about to launch from the flight deck of the* Ticonderoga *was taken sometime in October 1944. By World War Two standards, these were big planes, weighing in at just over 16,600 lbs. fully loaded.*

*This close-up profile of the port side of the* Ticonderoga *was taken on August 30, 1944. In this image, details of the support structure of the deck-edge elevator are visible, as well as the those of the island. The small boat hanging just aft of the deck-edge elevator is one of the two 26 ft. motor whaleboats carried. Just above that are the baskets attached to the flight deck edge which contain the floater nets. These were a life saving device. Also visible along the flight deck edge are the ships complement of rectangular 25-man life rafts. The US Navy made provision for life saving flotation for all crew members aboard ship. Just below the 26 ft. motor whaleboat is one of the ship's accommodation ladders.*

*This October 1944 photograph was taken as a F6F Hellcat prepares to take off from the* Ticonderoga. *This action took place while "Tico" was training her air group in Hawaiian waters prior to steaming to Ulithi to join Carrier Division 6, part of Task Force 38.*

Ticonderoga's *fighter squadron VF-80 prepares to take off for strikes against Luzon in the Philippines on November 13, 1944. Note that the F6F Hellcat fighters were armed with six rockets per plane, for attacks on the docks and shipping in Manila Harbor.*

*This image is an alternate to one of the more famous photographs of the US Navy during the World War Two period, often titled "Murderer's Row". The carriers in this image from front to back were* USS Was

orktown CV-10, Hornet CV-12, *and* Ticonderoga CV-14, *taken on December 8, 1944 from on board the fifth* Essex *class aircraft carrier to line up as part of that famous group at Ulithi,* USS Hancock CV-19.

"Tico" *crewmen towing 1,000 lb. bombs to their aircraft during the November 1944 raids on Luzon.*

*The image at the top is of shrapnel damage to a TBM Avenger. The lower image is of a F6F Hellcat in the foreground and a SB2C Helldiver just beyond on* Ticonderoga's *flight deck.*

Ticonderoga *after her second kamikaze hit, healing over while maneuvering in formation with* Essex. *Smoke continued to poor out from the hangar deck from the results of the first hit, but the fires were under control at the time this photograph was taken.*

*Both of the photographs on this page were taken on January 21, 1945, in the South China Sea while operating with TF-38 during strikes on Japanese installations on Formosa. The primary image on this page is of the* Ticonderoga *just after her initial kamikaze hit on the forward flight deck. Note the aft flight deck packed with aircraft. Forty minutes later another kamikaze struck her on the forward island structure. At the end of the day, 143 crewmen lost their lives and 202 were injured, making this the darkest day in* Ticonderoga's *entire career. This photograph was taken from the stern of the light cruiser* USS Biloxi CL-80.

Ticonderoga *seen after her February-April repair and refit at Puget Sound Naval Shipyard on the day of completion, April 20, 1945. She was painted in a new camouflage, Ms. 21, which was an overall Navy Blue (5-N). She also had her complement of quad 40 mm mounts increased by seven.*

*A Landing Signal Officer (LSO) guides returning aircraft onto the flight deck.*

*40 mm quadruple anti-aircraft mount and crew defending the warship.*

*Aircraft prepare to take off during the attacks upon Luzon, the Philippines.*

*Both of the images on this page of the* "Tico" *were taken on October 27, 1945, as the warship arrived at Tacoma, Washington with approximately 1,000 US soldiers and sailors returning home after the cessation of hostilities. During her early 1945 repair and refit at the Puget Sound Naval Shipyard,* CV-14 *had an upgrade to her radar, some of the antennas seen in these and the photographs on page 28. The most noticeable of these is the large round antenna for the SK-2 air search radar replacing the large square SK atop the island structure. The* Ticonderoga *was at Tacoma for the National Navy Day celebration the next day, but was sent down the coast to San Francisco for alterations to accommodate 4,000 passengers for the "Magic Carpet" voyages, returning US service personnel to the United States.*

SE2 BREMERTON,Wash.,Apr.23-Big "MOTHBALL FLEET" AT MOORAGE-These inactivated ships,described by Navy officials as largest "mothball fleet" of major vessels at any navy yard,lie at naval shipyard piers here. Front to rear carriers,Essex,Ticonderoga,Yorktown,Lexington,Bunker Hill. Left background, battleships,cruisers,destroyers; extreme center background,carrier Bon Homme Richard. (AP WIREPHOTO)vh61300tms

*The two images on this page are of the* Ticonderoga *during her Western Pacific Tours (WestPac) during 1960 and 1961. The smaller of the two photographs was taken while at Manila, the Philippines, sometime during 1961. The admirals barge, a 40 ft. Personnel Boat Mk. 1 was being lowered into the water. The primary image on this page was taken during 1960, with her air group parked on the flight deck. Note the modified Mk. 37 director on the aft end of the island structure. The radar antenna mounted atop that unit was for the Mk. 25 fire control radar for the remaining 5 in. AA mounts.*

Two more images from the flight deck of CVA-14 during the WestPac Tour during 1960-61.

*October 1954,* Ticonderoga, *fresh out of the New York Naval Shipyard from a major reconstruction. She would then be reclassified as an "Attack Aircraft Carrier", with the new hull number abbreviation* CVA-14. *Her reconstruction was labeled as SCB-27C, which was an abbreviation for "Ship Characteristic Board", while the number referred to the group of ships to be modernized. This modernization included increasing the beam to 103 ft. at the waterline with hull bulges, strengthening the flight deck to handle the weight of jet aircraft, installation of larger and more powerful steam catapults, and the installation of stronger flight deck arresting wires. Other modifications included the removal of all the twin 5 in. turrets, relocation of the open 5 in. DP mounts, conversion of the elevators (lifts) to make them larger and more powerful to handle jet aircraft, removal of side armor belt, increased aviation fuel storage capacity, and a major modification to the island structure to handle the demands of operating the new jet aircraft.*

# USS TICONDEROGA CVA-14

CVA-14 *at anchor in Guantanamo Bay, Cuba in February 1955, on her post-refit shakedown cruise.*

*This photograph was taken on June 2, 1955, while the* CVA-14 *was dry docked for final alterations at the New York Naval Shipyard.*

*The image above is of the 3in./50cal. twin automatic AA mounts, installed on the* Ticonderoga *during this modernization. This weapon was the replacement for the 40 mm quad AA mount. Below is a photograph of the Mk. 56 director which was used for fire control for the 3in. and as a back-up for the aircraft carrier's 5in. mounts.*

*An F8U Crusadar from the VA-25 Squadron is in the process of being launched from the flight deck catapult, while another is about to be hooked up to the starboard catapult, in this image dated sometime in 1969. The aircraft in the foreground was an A-7B.*

*Note the different colored shirts worn by the flight deck crew. Each color stood for an area of operation on the flight deck. Yellow is for plane handling officers & plane directors, red is for ordnance, green is for catapult crew & arresting crew, purple is for fuel, white is for safety officers, blue is for aircraft handling crew & chock men, and brown is for plane captains.*

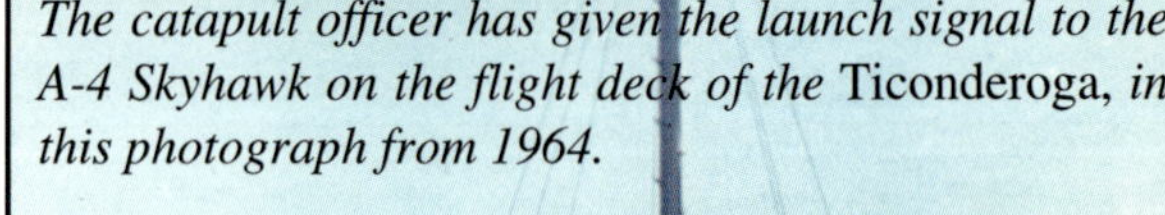

*A pair of A-4Fs over the* Ticonderoga, *sometime during 1968. These were from the VA-23 Squadron.*

*The catapult officer has given the launch signal to the A-4 Skyhawk on the flight deck of the* Ticonderoga, *in this photograph from 1964.*

*The primary image on this page is of the island structure aboard the* Ticonderoga, *while that ship was at anchor in Manila Bay, sometime in the mid 1960s. Note the large number of antennas for radar systems.*

*The photograph above is of the front of the bridge, or "Island", taken in the mid-1960s, while the ship was at anchor in Manila Bay, the Philippines. Note that the face of the bridge was painted black.*

CVA-14 USS Ticonderoga, *Hampton Roads, VA, departing the Norfolk Naval Shipyard, mid-1954, en route to Guantanamo Bay, Cuba, on her shakedown cruise in the Caribbean Sea. A small complement of aircraft was carried aboard to test the launching and take-off facilities on the carrier.*

SM

*An A4D can be seen making a landing aboard the* Ticonderoga *after a simulated strike on targets during her operational readiness inspection. This photograph was taken on January 18, 1963.*

*Quite possibly one of the best times had by any of the crews aboard the* Ticonderoga *during her entire career was the 1965 USO Tour, hosted by none other than Bob Hope, pictured above right, along with comedian Jerry Cologna. The "Go-Go" boot wearing beauty dancing with the enthusiastic sailors in the image to the left was showgirl Joey Heatherton, adding a little Christmas cheer for the "Tico's" crew along with the other celebrities on that USO Tour in December 1965, while the warship steamed off the coast of Vietnam in the South China Sea.*

*US Marines muster for inspection on board the* Ticonderoga *during December 1955, while on her Mediterranean deployment through July 1956. The small inset photograph to the right is of one of the open motor launches carried aboard* CVA-14 *to ferry personnel back and forth to shore, as seen in this image from late 1954 while "Tico" was on her shakedown cruise to Guantanamo Bay, Cuba.*

*This photograph is of the first Grumman F9F-8 Cougar to be catapulted from the deck of the* Ticonderoga *in January 1955.*

*This photograph, dated December 23, 1955, is of a Vought F7U-3 Cutlass about to launched from the flight deck of the* "Tico" *near the start of her Mediterranean deployment.*

*The* Ticonderoga *arrived at Pearl Harbor, Hawaii, on February 7, 1969, at the beginning of her fifth combat deployment to Vietnam.*

*Both of the images on this page are of the* Ticonderoga *in the final stages of her second reconstruction, taken in March 1957. This modification was known as SCB-125, and included the installation of the angled light deck, fitting of the "Hurricane" bow, dual arrestor wires, enlarging the forward elevator, installation of air-conditioning, stronger crash barriers, and improvements to flight control areas in the island structure. This reconstruction took place from August 17, 1956, through April 1, 1957, at the Norfolk Naval Shipyard.*

*The Photograph to the left is of the "Tico" at anchor in Yokosuka Bay, Japan, while on her WestPac Deployment during December 1957.*

*In the image above, the Jolly Roger pirate flag flies from the mast head of the* Ticonderoga, *as "Neptunus Rex" takes command as the ship proceeds across the Equator. The crew who have not crossed the Equator previously are known as Polly Wogs and will have to go before King Neptune's Court and become indoctrinated. By order of King Neptune, this will include a complete body smear of grease, a dunk in the brine pool and a rubber hose whipping. This photograph was taken in April 1957.*

*The two photographs on this page of the* Ticonderoga *were taken in 1960, below, and 1961, left. Both were taken while* CVA-14 *was operating out of her home port of San Diego, California. In the image to the left, the* Ticonderoga *was passing Point Loma. The "Tico" was departing San Diego in both of these images en route to her WestPac Cruises, stopping at ports like Pearl Harbor, Yokosuka & Sasebo, Japan, Subic Bay, the Philippines, and Hong Kong.*

*Both of the bow photographs on this page were taken in Japanese waters, with the image above taken in Yokosuka Harbor in December 1957 and the image to the right in 1960. Note the great number of radar antennas on the island structure. The very large antenna above the starboard side of the island in the photograph to the right was for an early version of the SPS-43 long range air search radar system. Note that the entire array of radar antennas, with the exception of the SPS-30 antenna, was painted gloss black. The SPS-30 radar was a pencil-beam height finding radar with an incredible range of at least 240 miles. That antenna was painted white. The flight deck was stained blue, but this tended to wear quickly, with the brown wood turning the overall color to purple. The deck markings were in both white and insignia yellow.*

*The image to the left is of one of the Ticonderoga's Douglas "Skyraider" ground attack aircraft, from Air Group 5, VA-52 Squadron. This type of ground attack aircraft was capable of carrying up to 8,000 lbs. of ordnance externally beneath the wings and fuselage. This type of aircraft also had folding wings to save room both in the hangar and on the flight deck, the fold seam visible on the right wing between the "N" and the "5". In September 1962, this Skyraider variant designation AD-6 was changed to A-1H. This particular aircraft was taxying towards the bow flight deck catapults in preparation for launching on August 4, 1964.*

*The photograph below is of the flight deck gang working to deploy the heavy duty nylon crash barrier netting on August 21, 1962. Note that much of the flight deck in this and many other photographs in this book from the 1960s is still covered with Douglas Fir wood planking.*

*All of the images on this page date from 1963-64. Above and below, the ordinance crews load Sidewinder air-to-air missiles on an F8U and a target drone on an F-3H, while the photograph to the right is of one of the Marine Corps UH-34D Seahorse helicopters embarking Marines during "Operation Wind Up" on October 21, 1963. In that image, the radar antenna to the extreme left was for the SPS-8 height finding radar, while the one above that was for the SPS-6 air search radar.*

*An A-3B of the VAH-4 Squadron flying over the* Ticonderoga, *sometime during the mid 1960s. This was the largest type of aircraft operated from this carrier.*

*An A-4F of the VA-25 Squadron flying over the* Ticonderoga, *sometime during the mid 1960s.*

*This aerial view of the* Ticonderoga *was taken while the ship was undergoing UnRep, sometime in 1965. Both the* CVA-14 *and the* Sumner *class destroyer,* USS Hubbard DD-748 *are replenishing their fuel bunkers from the oiler between them while underway at sea.*

*Both of the photographs on this page are also of the* Ticonderoga *while either refueling above, or below resupplying. In the top image, a Gearing class destroyer,* USS Basilone DD-824, *was also refueling at the same time as the* CVA-14. *In the lower image the supply ship was the* USS Wrangell AE-12, *an ammunition ship. Note the aircraft that was just launched in the lower image. Both photographs were taken while the "Tico" was operating off the coast of Vietnam.*

*The photograph above is of the starboard side aft, with the crew about to lift one of the ship's boats back aboard, sometime during 1963. The boat was a 50 ft. Non-Magnetic Utility Boat and was stowed inside the hangar bay.*

*The photograph to the left is of the forward portion of the island structure, showing the bridge and much of the detail of the hull on the starboard side while* "Tico" *was in the process of UnRep. This took place in the western Pacific Ocean during 1964.*

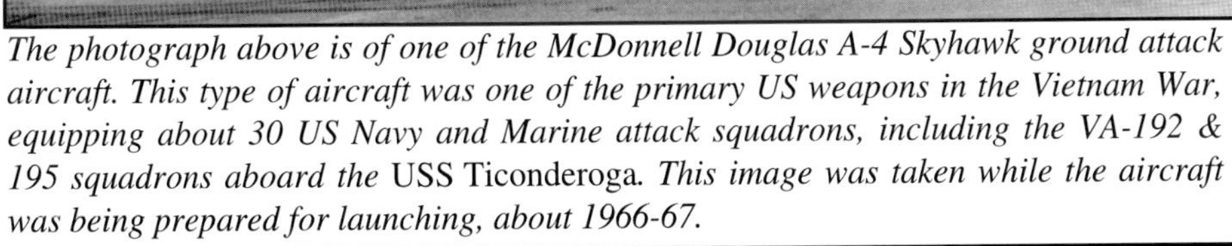
*The photograph above is of one of the McDonnell Douglas A-4 Skyhawk ground attack aircraft. This type of aircraft was one of the primary US weapons in the Vietnam War, equipping about 30 US Navy and Marine attack squadrons, including the VA-192 & 195 squadrons aboard the* USS Ticonderoga. *This image was taken while the aircraft was being prepared for launching, about 1966-67.*

*The image above is of one of the F8E fighters on an elevator about to be raised up to the flight deck during 1969, the year of* Ticonderoga's *fifth combat deployment to Vietnam.*

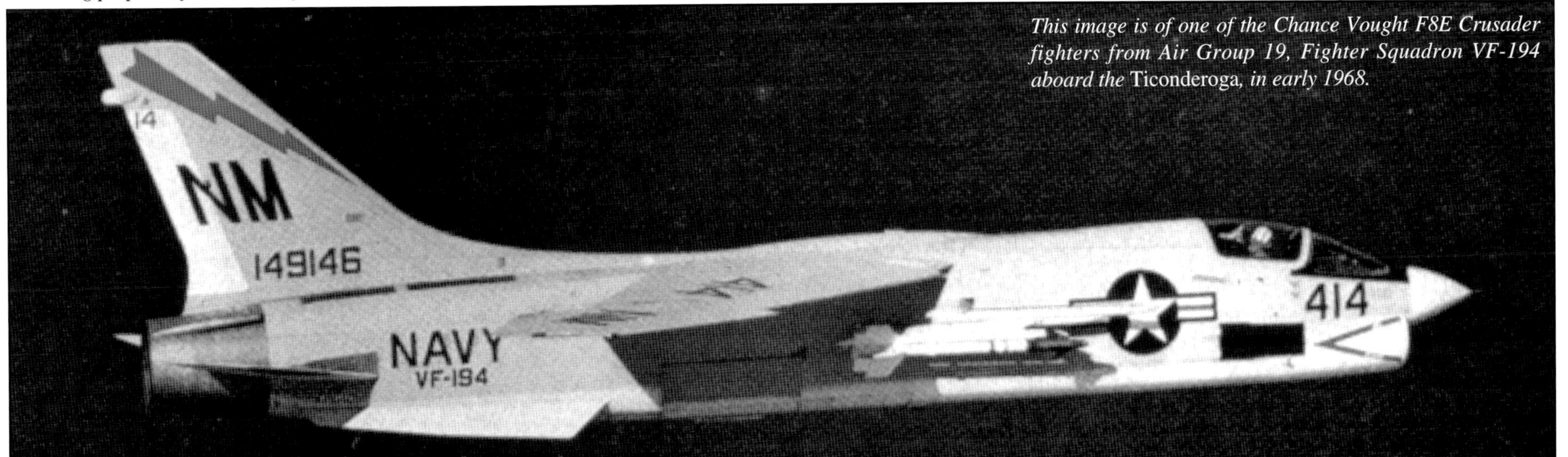

*This image is of one of the Chance Vought F8E Crusader fighters from Air Group 19, Fighter Squadron VF-194 aboard the* Ticonderoga, *in early 1968.*

*The image above is of some of the flight deck action during 1969, off the coast of Vietnam. Two A-7Bs from VA-25 were preparing to launch for air strikes against targets deep into Communist North Vietnam.*

*In the image to the right, an A-4 is on the deck edge elevator, or lift, about to be raised up to the flight deck and prepared for launching on a strike mission. This image was taken during 1966-67 period aboard the* Ticonderoga.

*The two photographs to the left side of this page are of the* Ticonderoga's *5 in. dual purpose mounts, taken in 1954 (top) and 1969 (bottom). By 1969 this weapon was kept as a last ditch defense against aircraft and small boats, which was entirely possible during the Vietnam War. In 1954 there were eight of these mounts fitted, but by the end of her career the "Tico" only mounted four.*

*The photograph to the right is of the* Ticonderoga *during a dry dock period in 1970-71, while undergoing another modernization, this time for anti-submarine warfare. She was re-classified as* "CVS-14" *at that time.*

"Tico" *in dry dock during her modernization to a* "CVS" *at the Long Beach Naval Shipyard during 1969.*

# USS TICONDEROGA CVS-14

*The lower photograph on the previous page of the* Ticonderoga *was an aerial view taken during 1970, while a flight of Grumman S-2E Tracker anti-submarine hunter/killer aircraft fly overhead.*

*Both of the photographs above are of the modified island structure, taken near the end of the modernization period in May 1970. Note that the Mk. 37 directors from the World War Two era were still retained on both of the fore and aft positions of the island. These were used to direct the four 5 in./38 cal. single dual purpose mounts retained and were aided by the Mk. 25 radar, the antenna mount atop each unit. The two large antennas atop the island structure were for the SPS-30 and 43 radar, described earlier. Note the extreme angle of the bridge windows to keep the glare to an absolute minimum. These were also tinted green.*

*Recommissioning ceremonies for the* Ticonderoga *in May of 1970 at the Long Beach Naval Shipyard in Long Beach, California. The large antenna mounted on the girder deck edge extension was for the Naval Tactical Data System. This was a radio link system for ships to send and receive tactical data in their area and was used for target selection, evaluation and weapons selection. This antenna was also seen mounted on the bow of large cruisers and the* Iowa *class battleships during this period.*

*This photograph was taken June 18, 1970, just after the* USS Ticonderoga *was recommissioned and redesignated as* CVS-14. *Her new role in the US Navy would be that of a submarine hunter and killer. The large antenna towards the stern on the starboard side was for ECCM, electronic counter-countermeasures. This system allows one adversary to collect electronic intelligence without allowing their potential opponents to know the use of their own ECM, or electronic countermeasures.*

CVS-14 USS Ticonderoga *in the process of UnRep, somewhere in the Western Pacific Ocean during February 1971. Note the ECM antenna protruding from the island structure just below the black SPS-43 antenna. This consisted of a transmitting and receiving antenna top, a receiver center and a jammer at the bottom. This same type of antenna array was on the bow of the* Iowa *class battleships of the same time period.*

*This photograph, dated April 17, 1972, was taken from one of the aircraft from* Ticonderoga's *air group for the recovery mission of Apollo 16. The aircraft pictured here were Grumman E-1B Tracer, twin engine aircraft, amidships with the large pancake radar dome atop the plane, Grumman S2 Tracker twin engine aircraft forward and Sikorsky SH-3G Sea King helicopters amidships.*

*The Apollo 16 splash down and recovery took place on April 27, 1972 at 0945, in what was the fastest recovery to date. From the time of splash down, the recovery mission was accomplished in just 38 minutes, taking the three astronauts Mattingly, Young and Duke from the water to the flight deck. Ticonderoga launched her recovery mission aircraft at 0840, At 0931, the Apollo 16 capsule "Casper" entered the Earth's atmosphere. The entire recovery went like clockwork.*

*The top left image is of the Underwater Demolition Team 12 (UDT-12) as they help the astronauts exit from the Apollo 16 capsule.*

*The lower left image is of the Apollo 16 capsule being lifted aboard the* Ticonderoga *later on the morning of April 27, 1972.*

*The photograph above is of the support sponson and the heavy lifting crane on the starboard side of* CVS-14.

*An aerial view of the* Ticonderoga, *taken two days after the Apollo 16 recovery mission, April 29, 1972. The crew has mustered on deck to form the "Apollo 16" image, and also formed "Tico 14" moments later. Note the layout of the flight deck markings. The bright lines were white, while the lines that look gray in this black and white photograph were yellow. The mostly wood covered flight deck was stained a very dark blue/gray.*

*This photograph of the* Ticonderoga *was taken on May 17, 1972, steaming out of San Diego, California. She then had Air Group 53 aboard and had resumed her role as an Anti-Submarine Warfare (ASW) vessel.*

*The image to the left is of the* CVS-14 *at sea in mid 1972, in the eastern Pacific Ocean.*

*Below is another photograph of the* "Tico" *departing San Diego as she passed Point Loma on May 17, 1972. One of the Sikorsky SH-3D Sea King helicopters is parked on the forward end of the flight deck and was "mothballed" for transport to another location. This type of helicopter was not only used in pairs for hunter/killer ASW role, but also for mine countermeasures, or minesweeping. The remaining aircraft aboard* CVS-14 *were from the Grumman S-2 Tracker family, which included the S-2E Tracker and the E-1B Tracer. Like the SH-3D helicopters, these aircraft were used for ASW purposes.*

*Both of the photographs on the previous page are from the recovery mission for the Apollo 17 splashdown, south of the Christmas Islands, just west of the island of Samoa in the south Pacific Ocean. The date was December 18, 1972. During this recovery mission, UDT-11 was the prime recovery team. Task Force 130 was the overall recovery force for Apollo 17, as well as the previous Apollo 16 mission. Apollo 17 astronauts were Cernan, Schmitt and Evans. The splashdown was at 0925, with the astronauts aboard by 1030. The image to the far left is of the Apollo 17 capsule after the parachutes opened at 0920. The image to the left is of the actual recovery just after splashdown, as is the image to the right. In that photograph, members of UDT-11 assist the astronauts to exit the capsule. This was a very tricky operation as the capsule was open at this time and in danger of flooding and sinking. This recovery mission for the* Ticonderoga *was from November 24 to December 28, 1972, the dates of departure and return to San Diego.*

*The image above is of the SH-3Ds of Squadron HS-8 aboard the* Ticonderoga *during the later half of 1972 while on her ASW cruise in the eastern Pacific Ocean. The aircraft in the background is a Grumman S-2E Tracker from Squadron VS-35.*

*The two photographs on the left side of this page pertain to the* Ticonderoga's *mission during the recovery of the Skylab II re-entry module. The upper image is of one of the "Tico's" helicopters, a Sikorsky SH-3G Sea King of Anti-Submarine Squadron HC-1, taken while practicing for the recovery mission. This would be the last deployment of the* Ticonderoga.

*VAW-111 aboard the* Ticonderoga *flew Grumman E-1B Tracer aircraft which provided an airborne communications relay network as its primary mission. This aircraft was used to track the Skylab II module as it entered the Earth's atmosphere. The aircraft pictured was actually a CIA transport.*

*The photograph below is a sad sight that no sailor wishes to see. The* Ticonderoga *was tied up at the San Diego Naval Air Station after being sold for scrapping on September 16, 1974, and was awaiting disposal.*

## General Statistics for USS Ticonderoga CV/CVA/CVS-14

### Displacement (tons - w/o aircraft)

| | | |
|---|---|---|
| 1944: | Light Ship | 24,100 |
| | Standard | 26,700 |
| | Full Load | 32,550 |
| 1945: | Full Load | 34,880 |
| 1954: | Full Load | 41,370 |
| 1970: | Full Load | 41,726 |

### Dimensions (feet)

| | | |
|---|---|---|
| 1944: | Length Overall | 888.5 |
| 1969: | Length Overall | 899.3 |
| 1944: | Beam (Flight Deck) | 147.7 |
| | Beam (Waterline) | 93.12 |
| 1969: | Beam (Flight Deck) | 191.9 |
| | Beam (Waterline) | 103.0 |
| 1944: | Draught (Full Load) | 27.50 |
| 1954: | Draught (Full Load) | 29.50 |
| 1969: | Draught (Full Load) | 30.33 |

### Machinery

| | |
|---|---|
| Boilers | 8 x Babcock & Wilcox |
| Engines | 4 sets Westinghouse Geared Turbines |
| Shafts | 4 |
| Ship Horse Power | 150,000 |
| Speed | 32 knots |
| Fuel Capacity | 6350 tons |

### Endurance

| | |
|---|---|
| 32 kts. | 4,100 nm. |
| 25 kts. | 10,700 nm. |
| 20 kts. | 14,100 nm. |
| 15 kts. | 16,900 nm. |

### Armament

| | |
|---|---|
| 1945 | 12 x 5 in./38 cal., 72 x 40 mm, 35 x 20 mm |
| 1955 | 8 x 5 in./38 cal., 28 x 3 in./50 cal. |
| 1959 | 8 x 5 in./38 cal., 8 x 3 in./50 cal. |
| 1972 | 4 x 5 in./38 cal. |

### Armor (inches)

| | |
|---|---|
| Belt | 4 to 2.5 |
| Flight Deck | none |
| Hangar Deck | 1.5 |
| Protective Deck | 1.5 |
| Bulkheads | 4 |
| Conning Tower | 1.5 |

### Complement

| | |
|---|---|
| 1944 | 268 Officers & 2,363 Men |
| 1959 | 354 Officers & 3,170 Men |
| 1970 | 115 Officers & 1,500 Men |

### Fire Control & Radar

| | |
|---|---|
| 1944: | 2 x Mk. 37 w/Mk. 4 Fire Control Radar (5 in.) |
| | 8 x Mk. 51 (40 mm) |
| | SG Surface Search Radar |
| | SC-2 & SK Air Search Radar |
| | SM-1 Fighter Control Radar |
| 1945: | 2 x Mk. 37 w/Mk. 12/22 Fire Control Radar (5 in.) |
| | 2 x Mk. 51 (5 in.) |
| | 12 x Mk. 51 (40 mm) |
| | 2 x Mk. 57 w/Mk. 29 Radar (5 in. & 40 mm) |
| | 4 x Mk. 63 w/Mk. 28 Radar (5 in. & 40 mm) |
| | SK-2 Air Search Radar |
| | SP Fighter Control Radar |
| 1955: | 2 x Mk. 37 w/Mk. 25 Fire Control Radar (5 in.) |
| | 4 x Mk. 56 w/Mk. 35 Fire Control Radar (3 in.) |
| | 4 x Mk. 63 w/Mk. 28 Radar (5 in. & 3 in) |
| | SC-2 Air Search Radar (1954-59) |
| | SPS-8A Height Finding Radar (1954-66) |
| | SPS-12 Air Search Radar (1954-66) |
| | SPS-30 Height Finding Radar (1966-73) |
| | SPS-43 Air Search Radar (1966-73) |
| 1969: | 1 x Mk. 37 w/Mk. 25 Fire Control Radar (5 in.) |
| | SPS-30 Height Finding Radar |
| | SPS-43 Air Search Radar |

## USS Ticonderoga Air Groups & Squadrons

| | | |
|---|---|---|
| **June 1944:** | Air Group 80 | VF-80(73 F6F); VFN-105(6 F6F-5N); VB-80(22 SB2C); VT-80(16 TBM). Caribbean shakedown, 117 aircraft total. |
| **January 1945:** | Air Group 80 | VF-80(68 F6F + 3 F6F-5N + 2 F6F-5P); VB-80(22 SB2C); VT-80(16 TBM). 111 aircraft total. |
| **February 1945:** | Air Group 7 | VF-7(F6F-5); VB-7(SB2C-3); VBF-7(F6F-5); VT-7(TBM-1C). Return to USA. |
| **May 1945:** | Air Group 87 | VF-87(52 F6F + 4 F6F-5N + 2 F6F-5P); VB-87(22 SB2C); VT-87(16 TBM). 96 aircraft total, Japanese Home Islands. |
| **February 1955:** | Air Group 6 | VF-74(F9F-8); VA-25(AD-6); VC-4(F2H-4); VC-12(AD-5W); HU-2(HUP-2). Caribbean shakedown. |
| **November 1955:** | Air Group 3 | VF-31(F2H-3); VF-32(F9F-8); VA-35(AD-6); VA-66(F7U-3); VAH-9(AJ-2); VC-12(AD-5W); VC-33(AD-5N/Q); VC-62(F2H-2P). Sixth Fleet - Mediterranean. |
| **October 1957:** | Air Group 9 | VF-91(FJ-3); VF-122(F3H-2N); VFP-61(F2H-2P); VA-93(A4D-1); VA-95(AD-7); VAH-2(A3D-2); VAW-11(AD-5W); VAAW-35(AD-5N); HU-1(HUP-3); GMGRU-1(FJ-3D). |
| **October 1958:** | Air Group ATG-1 | VF-52(F2H-3); VF-112(F3H-2M); VFP-61(F9F-8P); VA-151(FJ-4B); VA-196(AD-6); VAH-2(A3D-2); VAW-11(AD-5W); VAAW(AD-5N); HU-1(HUP-2). Seventh Fleet. |
| **March 1960:** | Air Group 5 | VF-51(F4D-1); VF-53(F3H-2); VA-52(AD-6); VA-55(A4D-2); VA-56(A4D-2); VAH-4(A3D-2); VAW-11(AD-5W). Seventh Fleet - Western Pacific. |
| **May 1961:** | Air Group 5 | VF-51(F8U-1); VF-53(F3H-2); VA-52(AD-6); VA-55(A4D-2); VA-56(A4D-2); VAH-4(A3D-2); VAW-11(WF-2); VAW-13(AD-5Q) VFP-61(F8U-1P). Seventh Fleet. |
| **September 1965:** | Air Group 5 | VF-51(F-8E); VF-53(F-8E); VFP-63(RF-8); VA-52(A-1H/J); VA-56(A-4E); VA-144(A-4C); VAH-4(A-3B); VAW-11(E-1B); VQ-1(EA-3B); HC-1(UH-2A/B). Seventh Fleet. |
| **October 1966:** | Air Group 19 | VF-191(F-8E); VF-194(F-8E); VFP-63(RF-8G); VA-52(A-1H/J); VA-192(A-4E); VA-195(A-4C); VAH-4(A-3B); VAW-11(E-1B); VQ-1(EA-3B); HC-1(UH-2A/B). Seventh Fleet. |
| **December 1967:** | Air Group 19 | VF-191(F-8E); VF-194(F-8E); VFP 63(RF-8A); VA-23(A-4F); VA-192(A-4F); VA-195(A-4C); VAH-4(KA-3B); VAW-111(E-1B); VAW-33(EA-1F); HC-1(UH-2A/B). Seventh Fleet. |
| **February 1969:** | Air Group 16 | VF-111(F-8H); VF-162(F-8J); VFP-63(RF-8G); VA-25(A-7B); VA-87(A-7B); VAW-111(E-1B); VAQ 130(EKA-3B); HC-1(UH-2C). Seventh Fleet. |
| **August 1970:** | Air Group 53 | VS-21(S-2E); VS-29(S-2E); VS-35(S-2E); VAW-111(E-1B); HS-6(SH-3A). Eastern Pacific. |
| **October 1970:** | Air Group 59 | VS-33(S-2E); VS-37(S-2E); VS-38(S-2E); VAW-111(E-1B); HS-4(SH-3D); HS-8(SH-3D). Eastern & Western Pacific. |
| **July 1971:** | Air Group 80 | VS-81(S-2E); VS-82(S-2E); VS-83(S-2E); VSF-86(A-4C); VAW-88(E-1B); HS-84(SH-3A); HS-85(SH-3A). Eastern Pacific. |
| **August 1971:** | Air Group 53 | VS-21(S-2E); VS-29(S-2E); VS-35(S-2E); VAW-111(E-1B); HS-2(SH-3A); HS-6(SH-3A). Eastern Pacific. |
| **October 1971:** | Air Group 59 | VS-33(S-2E); VS-37(S-2E); VS-38(S-2E); VAW-111(E-1B); HS-4(SH-3D); HS-8(SH-3D). Eastern Pacific. |
| **March 1972:** | AS-16 Recovery | VAW-111(E-1B); VR-30(C-1A); HC-1(SH-3G). Apollo 16 Recovery Mission - South Pacific. |
| **May 1972:** | Air Group 53 | VS-21(S-2E); VS-29(S-2E); VS-33(S-2E); VS-35(S-2E); VS-38(S-2E); VAW-111(E-1B); HS-4(SH-3A); HS-8(SH-3A). Eastern Pacific. |
| **November 1972:** | AS-17 Recovery | VAW-111(E-1B); VR-30(C-1A); HC-1(SH-3G). Apollo 17 Recovery Mission - South Pacific. |
| **June 1973:** | SL-2 Recovery | VAW-111(E-1B); VR(C-1A); HC-1(SH-3G). Skylab II Recovery Mission - Eastern Pacific. |

# REFERENCES


**Aircraft Carriers of the US Navy**
S. Terzibaschitsch, Conway Maritime Press, 1980
**Anatomy of the Ship - Aircraft Carrier INTREPID**
J. Roberts, Naval Institute Press, 1982
**The Essex Aircraft Carriers**
A. Faltum, Nautical & Aviation Publishing, 1996
**Essex-Class Carriers**
A. Raven, Naval Institute Press, 1988
**Naval Radar**
N. Friedman, Conway Maritime Press, 1988
**Naval Weapons of WWII**
J. Campbell, Conway Maritime Press, 1985
**Register of Ships of the U. S. Navy 1775-1990**
K. Bauer & S. Roberts, Greenwood Press, 1991
**U.S. Aircraft Carriers**
N. Friedman, Naval Institute Press, 1983
**United States Fleet Carriers of World War II**
R. Humble, Blandford Press, 1984
**U.S. Naval Weapons**
N. Friedman, Naval Institute Press, 1985
**United States Navy Aircraft**
G. Swanborough & P. Bowers, Naval Institute Press, 1990


# RESOURCES

**U. S. Naval Historical Center**
Building 57, 805 Kidder Breese St. SE,
Washington Navy Yard, Washington DC, 20374-2571
(202)433-2765 • Web site: www.history.navy.mil

**U. S. National Archives - Archives II**
8601 Adelphi Rd., College Park, MD. 20740-6001
(301)713-6800 • Web site: www.nara.gov

**U. S. Naval Institute**
291 Wood Rd., Annapolis, MD 21402-5034
(800)233-8764 • Web site: www.usni.org

# ACKNOWLEDGMENTS


Classic Warships
would like to express its gratitude to the following individuals
**Louis Parker • Don Montgomery • Steve Barker**
**A. D. Baker III • Don Preul & Jeanne Pollard**
**Ed Finney, Rob Hanshew & Chuck Haberlein, Jr.**
**@ US Naval Historical Center**
**All the nice ladies on the 5th. floor @ Archives II**
***The Following* Ticonderoga *Veterans -***
**Francis Beams • D. Johnson • Alfred Llach • R. W. Lee**
**John Lunsford • John Rochford • John Slavin**
**Edgar Trotter, Jr. • R. E. Waugh • Donald Westover**


# WARSHIP PICTORIAL SERIES

at the time of this printing

W. P. # 4 USS Texas BB-35
W. P. # 7 New Orleans Class Cruisers
W. P. # 9 Yorktown Class Carriers
W. P. #10 Indianapolis & Portland
W. P. #12 Benson/Gleaves Class Destroyers
W. P. #14 USS Wichita CA-45
W. P. #17 IJN Myoko Class Cruisers
W. P. #18 USS New Mexico BB-40
W. P. #19 KM Bismarck
W. P. #20 HMS Hood
W. P. #21 KM Prinz Eugen
W. P. #22 USS Ticonderoga CV/CVA/CVS-14
W. P. #25 IJN Yamato Class Battleships

*The subject of Warship Pictorial #25 is the Imperial Japanese Navy* Yamato *Class Battleships, with the* Yamato *pictured here on her trials, October 30, 1941, in the Inland Sea.*

**Front Cover:** *CV-14* in May 1944. This is a colorized black and white photograph.

**Back Cover:** *CVA-14* circa 1970-72.